INKY WINKY SPIDER

COLORS BY THE BAY

2003 By Cyndi Sue

Illustrations By Kevin Riley
With Brian Parks 2006. All rights reserved.

Published By New Vision Entertainment LLC

Dedication

Thank you family and freinds for encouraging me throughout this journey. My grateful appreciation to "talent scout" Lori LaBrecque, who acknowledged my idea and provided for my entrée. Special thanks to Publishers Jim and Maura Sweeney for believing in me and offering their unwavering support to transform my dream into a reality. Finally, thank you Kevin Riley for your incredible artistic gift which has brought Inky Winky to life.

– Cyndi Sue

ISBN 0-9778310-0-0

Copyright@2003 by Cyndi Sue

Illustrations by Kevin Riley
with Brian Parks 2006. All rights reserved.

Published by New Vision Entertainment LLC

Printed in the U.S.A. 2006

Inky Winky Spider was looking in the sky.
As he waited for his friends a rainbow caught his eye.

"Oh, hi, my little friends,
I wanted you to know,
That we can have some fun
making colors for a show.
It's a color show," said Inky,
"That's starting By the Bay,
where we can make our colors
in a very special way."

"Yes, we'll all go with you," those little spiders said,
and down the path they went, moving quickly straight ahead.

Down, Down the path they went
skipping on their way,
Taking colored ink pens
for their very Busy Day.

They finally reached the water
where the show was going to start,
And there they found some easels
and began to do their art.

Inky Winky started with his favorite color Blue.
He made a Deep Blue sky Plus white clouds were added too.

"I love, I love my colors," Inky winked and spoke once more,
And he danced around the easel like he never did before.

Then one of Inky's friends who loved the color green,
Drew tall green blades of grass with brown spiders in between.

"We love, we love our colors," those little spiders said.
Then they all started spinning and the ink fell on their heads.

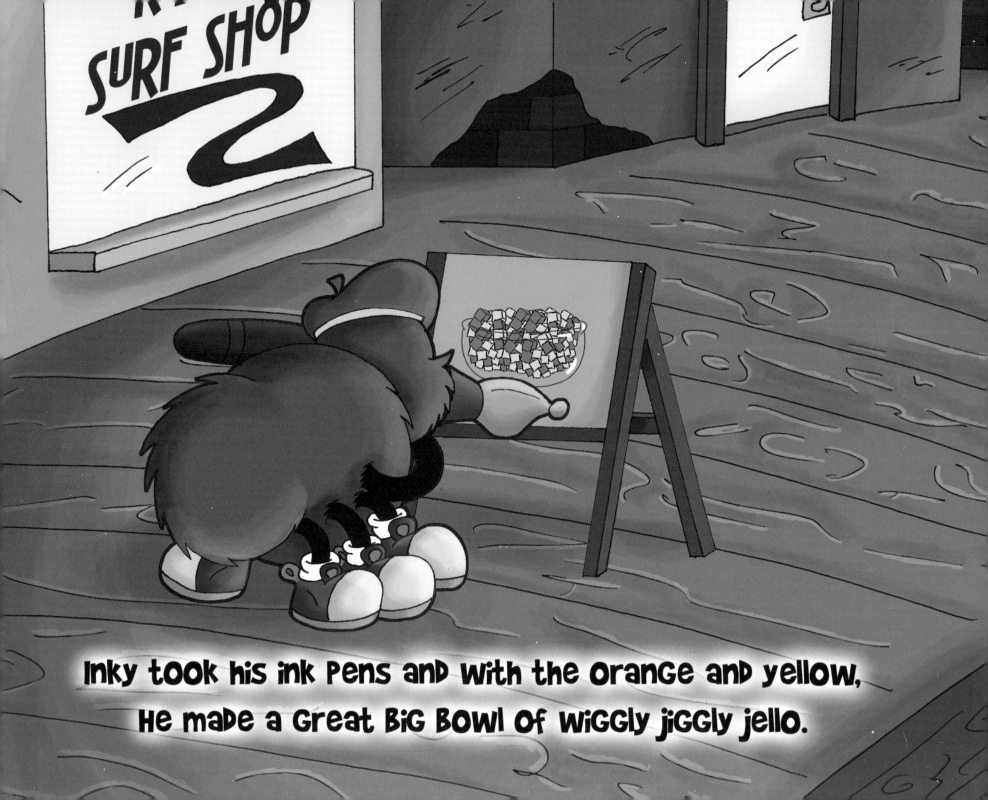

Inky took his ink pens and with the orange and yellow,
He made a great big bowl of wiggly jiggly jello.

NOW INKY WINKY'S little friend Began to color too
And with the Pink and Purple, she made a Big Bright shiny shoe.

AND WERE SO PROUD OF what they made
they all jumped in the Bay.

Back to painting they did go, and Inky now would start,
With a deep, dark shade of red, he made a great big giant heart.

Inky Winky's little friends were gathered there to say,
That Inky Winky's Drawing was the highlight of the day.

Inky looked up toward the sky and it was Black and Gray.
He knew the rain was sure to come and that would end their Day.

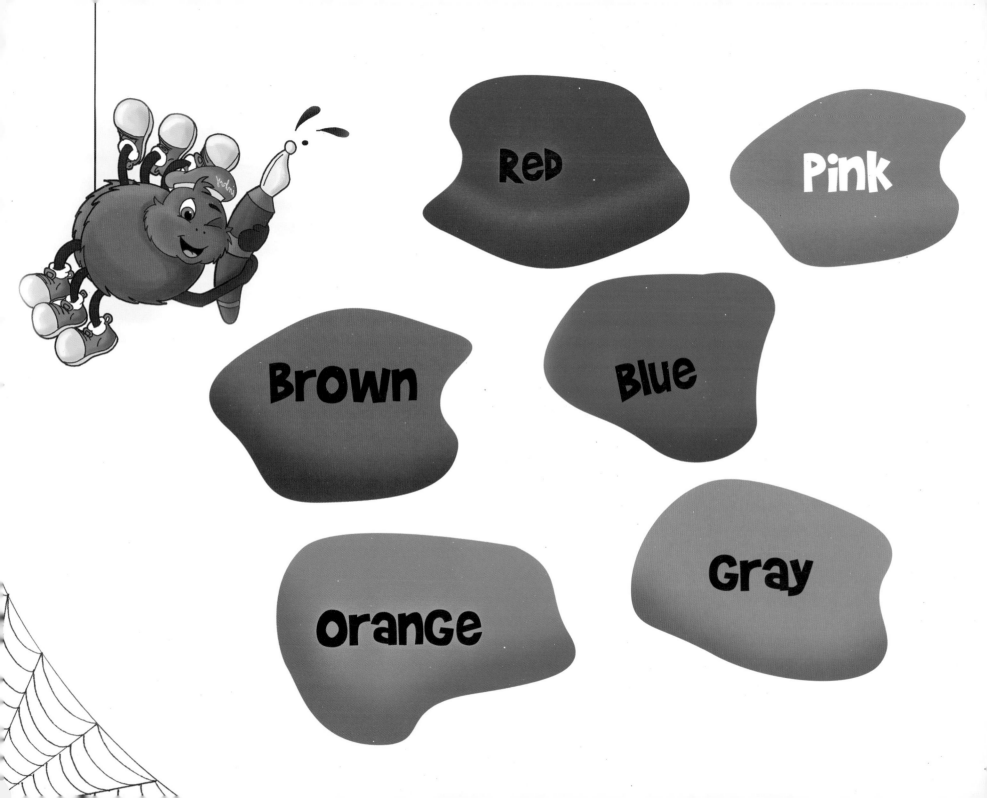

Yellow

Green

Black

White

Purple